Clean-Up Day

written by Catherine James
illustrated by Abby Carter

HARCOURT BRACE & COMPANY

Orlando Atlanta Austin Boston San Francisco Chicago Dallas New York
Toronto London

Today my family cleaned up the whole house. Some things were given away or sold or fixed or thrown away.

3

First I cleaned my closet and packed up my old clothes. My mom will take these clothes to my little cousin Susanna.

5

In the playroom, my brother and I decided which toys we could give away. The twins across the street will like the toys in this box.

7

Mom and Grandma worked all week getting ready for a yard sale. Lots of people have come to buy things we don't need anymore.

9

In the afternoon Dad gave away his old bike. It will be as good as new when Mr. Young puts new tires on it.

11

At the end of the day, everyone swept, washed, and packed. The house looked great.

13

With some of the money from the yard sale, we had a pizza party for dinner. We didn't throw away any pizza!

15

With the rest of the money from the yard sale, we decided to buy a few things. And hopefully we'll never have to throw away these.